The great Hand Book *of* Quotes!

~ *Israelmore Ayivor*

www.amazon.com/author/israelmore

The great Hand Book of Quotes!

Thank you for purchasing this book!

The great Hand book of Quotes!
Copyright © *2013*- Israelmore Ayivor.

All rights reserved.

Email: israelive@live.com
Phone: (+233)0244920845/ (+233)0209060903
Website: www.IsraelmoreAyivor.com

SHARE IT FREELY WITH YOUR FRIENDS

Please Kindly LIKE my Facebook page: (www.facebook.com/israelmoreayivor)

Let's be friends: *My Facebook Username: Israelmore Ayivor My twitter Username: Israelsrael My Google+ Username: Israelmore Ayivor*

Feel FREE to visit my Amazon shelf for my books: www.amazon.com/author/israelmore or Goodreads quoteland for my quotes: www.goodreads.com/author/quotes/7023141

Live Life So Well…

www.amazon.com/author/israelmore

The great Hand Book of Quotes!

Remember, this Book is Updated every 2 months. Purchase your updated version for additional quotes!

Send e-mail to: info@israelmoreayivor.com for updates!

www.amazon.com/author/israelmore

The great Hand Book of Quotes!

Enjoy the trends of Quotes …

from Number 1 till….

www.amazon.com/author/israelmore

The great Hand Book of Quotes!

1. There comes some special times that you got to keep "impossibility thinkers" behind you and walk with those are prepared to go forward with you because that is the only option to keep you going!

2. The role that people play in your life can determine how far you can go. Football Coaches do play football matches; their attitudes toward the game in times of tendencies of losing can cause a change in the scores of the games!

3. Never allow the spirit of complacency to possess you. The excellence of today is the mediocrity of tomorrow. So why should you sit idle after those trophies?

4. Never see that little trophy you have won and predict the end to your determination for greater laurels. Keep going higher no matter how high you have already gone.

5. People who should have been soaring as eagles are perching as weaver birds all because they are complacent with the little they have accomplished! If you have accomplished 100, it means you can get to 1,000. And why not 10,000? You can!

6. Selfish leaders who are quick to hoard facilities for themselves and their families cannot make the world a better place for you and for me! It also means if we are also going to make the world a better place for others, we must look for needs that should be solved, not opponents that should be dealt with!

www.amazon.com/author/israelmore

The great Hand Book of Quotes!

7. If we are determined to change the world, then we must be willing to be and stand for a leadership that targets its opportunities rather than the leadership that targets its opposition!

8. Don't frown when you get hurt; never curse when you are disappointed! You are only adding pepper to your lemon after all. That is already a bitter solution. Never let the sun go down on that bitter solution; it will get fermented and smell badly! Think about it... It's not drinkable!

9. When life gives you a lemon, make lemonade! Lemon is bitter, but lemonade is better; It's sweet! Add your own favours to the bitter stories that come to meet you unexpectedly. They will become sweeter!

10. When life gives you a mess, change it into a message! Let the world know that message. Let it transform people; let it not mess you up. It's may have been designed like that, so that your worst miseries will turn to become an interesting history!

11. Our critics make us strong!
    Our fears make us bold!
    Our haters make us wise!
    Our foes make us active!
    Our obstacles make us passionate!
    Our losses make us wealthy!
    Our disappointments make us appointed!
    Our unseen treasures give us a

The great Hand Book of Quotes!

known peace!

Whatever is designed against us will work for us!

12. The economy of your country shall never determine the size of your three square meals if you know you can rise against and above all limitations! The climatic emergencies in the weather shall never determine your survival rates if you know you are above their standards!

13. You may have been born on the rubbish damp. But be careful not to believe that the rubbish damp was born in you! Your environment may try to set conditions that may attempt their fingers on crippling you. But you got to stand and say "I thank you Lord that I am rising against and above my limitations"

14. Take a stand; go for the right choice. Don't just sit for anything; stand for something. Be specific because sometimes, when the meaning is not clear, there us absolutely no meaning!

15. Don't just settle for surviving; Settle to make impacts. Life is deliberate; It's about making a difference!

16. That fact that you are true child of God doesn't mean you will find gold on the floor when sweeping. You got to dig up the gold!

www.amazon.com/author/israelmore

The great Hand Book of Quotes!

17. If you live your life to chance, you can't make a change. Chance may favour a prepared mind, but it doesn't create change! Will does so.

18. It is said that if you want to change the world, take pen and write. I want to add that if you want to maintain that change, then be the ruler to rule the pen's lines. True rulers are true leaders; they maintain a change!

19. God wants to use you as a divine showroom, where the poor, the wearied and the depressed will find comfort and recreation! You got to be kind. It's a sign that you have conquered greed!

20. Success is reserved for you if you persevere; it's not deserved by you if you are indolent!

21. You have been complaining so long about your labour pains. It's time to show us your baby! What at all have you been dreaming about that long? Let's see it and give it a name!

22. A clear passion, a resolute determination, a can-do spirit; these are the rods for creating a great mark!

23. Big dreams are marathons. Big actions are marathons of marathons! Waiters don't deserve it; Quitters don't get it!

24. You cannot enjoy true love in relationship if you don't add honest flavours to it. You can genuinely maintain what you can sincerely entertain!

www.amazon.com/author/israelmore

The great Hand Book of Quotes!

25. "Your potentials are called POTENTIALS because they are POTENT. Don't make them IMPOTENT by being IMPATIENT. Make an IMPACT".

26. Nothing comes as an accomplishment instantly. Success does not come overnight. Patience is the key! Grow up and be the tree; but remember it takes dry and wet seasons to become a fruit bearer, achiever and impact maker!

27. No matter how potent your talents are, they remain to be out of use until you take time to develop them to their optimum level. This calls for preparation. Through preparation, personal branding, consistent exposure and productive connections, you set up a condition for your dreams to flourish and bear fruits!

28. It's when the seed grows up that it is known as the tree. Nobody calls the "seedlings" as "trees" and no seedling is even useful because it doesn't produce fruits! You got to grow up!

29. The beauty of your mind depends on the "make-ups" you use to feed it. A "can-do-spirit" is the best cosmetic. It never fades your mental beauty!

30. Your mind controls your actions and that means when your mind gives you designed thoughts, your actions too are going to be designed actions!

www.amazon.com/author/israelmore

The great Hand Book of Quotes!

31. Your mental make-ups are the contents of your everyday thinking; they carry a charge that can either transform, reform or deform you. Watch your thoughts, they determine your life!

32. Don't rush to design your face to look beautiful, attractive and charming. Rather, be quicker to decorate your mind to appear as goal-oriented, passion-embedded and action-driven.

33. Never leave your life plan to be determined by people who are not going where you are going. For the sake of your dreams and also for the sake of the people God created to benefit from your God-give talents, stay away from toxic people. Mount the shoulder giants and see farther ahead!

34. Keep it calm and watch the company you keep. It's either a a red card or a green card you are holding. One guides you to go on, and the other makes you give up on scoring your goals.

35. You cannot climb up to a true leadership position unless you use the ladder of integrity!

36. Until you get enough of enough, the "enough" that is never enough, you dare not quit! If your good is better, your better can be best; your best too can become excellent!

www.amazon.com/author/israelmore

The great Hand Book of Quotes!

37. God has not given us the spirit of fear. So imagine where your fear coming from. It's from somewhere else!

38. I am convinced that "all ladies are not the same". Some have pretty faces, others have beautiful characters. Some have facial make-ups, others have mental make-ups!

39. "Don't compare yourself to other Christians. Compare yourself to Christ. He is the one you follow. He is the one other Christians too follow".

40. God gave the seed, but he wants the fruits back. Pick the seeds up. Plant the best ones. He promised the rain. It will be a bumper harvest!

41. Compass rules direction; Decision rules life!

42. Real kings and queens are people whose heads are crowned with dreams as they sit on the throne of passion. They rule with visions in the regalia of inspirations!

43. Go to where ever dreamland you decide on. But go with passion hand-in-hand. You will never be tired on the way!

44. There are no big men and big women. There are small people with big dreams and big passions!

45. The way to the hall of failure passes through the chamber of indecision. The way to the hall of success passes

www.amazon.com/author/israelmore

The great Hand Book of Quotes!

through the chamber of decision. Success and failure are deliberately won!

46. The way into the hall of success always passes through the chamber of decision. Decide to be a success; success is deliberate!

47. Your life success is well designed by the mental transformation you experience. That mental transformation guides you to construct powerful decisions. You can't live life so well without mental make-ups.

48. Indecision is the reluctance or inability to pass a judgment on an issue under consideration. Indecision means you have come to crossroads and you cannot make your mind.

49. Decision decides destiny. What God wants you to become is the very person you decide to become when led by God's spirit.

50. Stop blaming people for not helping you to solve your problems. The question is simple "are they the ones in the problem with you"? People may teach you, people may advise you, people may inspire you, but it takes YOU to go the extra mile and make an indelible impact!

51. You cannot do anything unless you allow your passion to motivate you. People may tell you, "you can do it", "you can make it" "it's possible" but when you tell yourself

The great Hand Book of Quotes!

always " I can't make it", it's your choice that rules everything!

52. Passionate people are always ready to stand for their dreams even if no one stand with them. They vote and vote alone for their dreams but never loss their nomination for excellent leadership!

53. Learn wider, grow wiser!

54. Save your mind from a premature death by always learning something new no matter your age! Think every day, but make sure it's not within the perimeter of the box!

55. Intellectual death is endemic in areas where people are not prepared to gain new information for development. Learning is the intervention!

56. The day you stop learning is the day you begin to die. Lack of knowledge is the fundamental principle for killing "live and kicking" dreams.

57. Learning is like the fuel that moves the machinery of your body towards it's destination of success. Shortage is possible, hence spare supply is necessary!

58. When you abbreviate your learning, you abbreviate your growth. Expand your knowledge and you keep growing taller and fatter than your limitations.

www.amazon.com/author/israelmore

The great Hand Book of Quotes!

59. Wisdom is the principal thing. The principle to discover the principal thing is "the fear of the Lord". Fear God and be wise.

60. When you are able to know the right thing, you are intelligent. But when you choose that right thing to do, you are wise. This means people can get money, education, marriage, and good health and not get wisdom. Wisdom is the number one gift for a Godly success.

61. Wisdom is the ability to make wise decisions and pursue them. The bible said "wisdom is the principal thing". This means it's the number one thing ever that you cannot bypass and expect to succeed!

62. You can do nothing without prayer and everything with it. Anything worth worrying about is something worth praying about.

63. Don't keep looking for "something" in the bag of "nothing". You will see the same thing again and again no matter how many times you repeat the look.

64. There are two types of patience. One is exercised in hard work and the other in idleness. Patience with hard work is the one that moves mountains. Patience in idleness moves nothing, not even cobwebs.

65. When the way is not clear, there is absolutely no way. "Wrong choices" are unarguably "no choices".

www.amazon.com/author/israelmore

The great Hand Book of Quotes!

66. Plan and plant your gifts. Pray and play your role. The harvest is assured when God manifests his anointing in your actions.

67. Don't despise the little steps you know you can take every day. There are tiny miracles in each and every one of them.

68. You destruct the attention the world gives you when you mistrust your own ability.

69. Superiority complex does not mean "pride" although it appears to be so in the eyes of those who want to see it so. When you feel a higher esteem over the obstacles you desire to surmount, you highly overcome them and can still count a reserved energy to spare!

70. People with inferiority intentions do not go after their dreams not because they can't go; but because their passion is not strong enough to turn the wheels of success...and there they go, becoming losers, defeated by their obstacles!

71. In every dream you pursue, you attract its respective version of opposition. Going back will not solve any problem; Regrets will not change anything either; Feeling of Superiority over every obstacle should be your priority!

72. A successful person's life is made up of a time when he gets out of bed, and a time he goes to bed; and in-between

The great Hand Book of Quotes!

them is filled up with a time that he makes sure something definitely happened!

73. Whatever you find to be very difficult for you, believe it that it's never difficult if you do something little about it every day!

74. Don't live by your thoughts only; live by your words also. Whatever plans you think about, affirm it in your mouth first, declare it and you will succeed in working it out! Words can be powerful!

75. The chance that you will become a master in something after the first attempt is neither here nor there. You don't get master's degree by attending school on the first day of your life! Time will tell, so you got to persist!

76. Majority of excuses are deliberate attempts to keep success far away. Eventually, the success goes away because that is the command "excuses" gave out; "pack and go"!

77. Never REJECT yourself due to the sins you have committed. REGRET will do nothing; REPENT and do something!

78. Keep negative people long metres away from you; their presence is a threat to your high self-esteem! Job, the man of God kept his wife afar before he could make it again!

www.amazon.com/author/israelmore

The great Hand Book of Quotes!

79. The emptiness of your pocket is not a recipe for you to discount the value of your passion!

80. The level of your self-control is measured as the difference between how you act when you have nothing and how you react when you have everything.

81. You can go with an empty pocket and come back heavy if you allow your passion to escort you!

82. Before someone will get the guts to monitor your life, he must get the keyboard of humility. To be a humble person, is a priority in leadership!

83. Not every hen lay eggs. Not every hen that lays eggs gets them hatched. Not everyone born with greatness becomes as such. Go, hatch your eggs.

84. We live for our dreams when we are alive. Our dreams live for us when we are gone!

85. You got the eggs in you; the world is fully ready to celebrate the chicks out of your laying labour. Never give up. Go and breed! Go and breed great dreams.

86. Never leave the egg in you not laid. Don't leave the laid eggs there not hatched. You deserve the best; you were created to use every gift in you!

The great Hand Book of Quotes!

87. You got the eggs in you; the world is fully ready to celebrate the chicks out of your laying labour. Never give up. Go and breed! Go and breed great dreams.

88. You cannot be responsible for some things that happen on earth. You may attempt to act, God alone will decide. Some things are mysteries!

89. If I am to choose between integrity and wealth, I will go for integrity because I believe that lack of integrity is the first killer of wealthiest dreams!

90. The size and height of the tree determines how heavy the ground will shake when it falls. The cassava tree falls and not even the pests in the forest are aware. The baobab tree falls and the whole forest looks empty! Such is human life!

91. People who make great impact are well remembered due to the empty seats that remain after their death. It takes time to fill the empty seats that are left unoccupied by people who walked great in great footprints.

92. Who regulates the heat of the sun? Who pays the bills of the energy we obtain from the sun? Leave all judgments to that man if you believe we all walk under that same sun!

93. Live life so well that, even if you die, the empty seats behind you will tell the story that, "yea, this soul did what God sent him/her to do". Give life and hope into your

The great Hand Book of Quotes!

family, village, community, country, continent and the world at large. You can do it!

94. The major factor that makes a great leader to fail emerge from the decision of people who surround him/her.

95. Your vehicle of leadership is fuelled by your willingness to learn. You can't lead if you can't learn!

96. You have no control over your growth or development. But you have a control on the direction of your growth and development! Go, grow towards impact directions!

97. One major factor that makes most achievers to fail is their ability to know where they are going and becoming unaware of what they will have to do when they get there!

98. Getting to the top should be a priority, but being aware of the reason for getting there should be the focus!

99. Great leaders are most wanted. They are most wanted for what they do with their gifts and talents. Their dreams are so unique in such a way that their presence becomes a source of hope and courage for others to thread on along. Why won't they look for them?

100. The best university in the world is neither Oxford nor Harvard. The best university is "youniversity". YOU got the lecture halls of thoughts in YOU! You got

The great Hand Book of Quotes!

everything you need to graduate with first class accomplishments put in you! YOU can do it!

101. If you see yourself as other people see you, it means you are lost, you don't know yourself and you have closed down a world class university of diligence!

102. Enroll your body, soul and spirit and engage your time to do what you know best. Dedicate yourself to the work at hand and you will be rewarded by the fruits you will bear!

103. My friends, life is so serious that if you are not aware of whom you are, your "youniversity" will be prestigious but unknown!

104. Idea lady is the ideal lady!

105. In the faculty of failure, mediocrity is never an optional course!

106. Whatever dream God gave to you is for the comfort of those God keeps around you!

107. Pesticide is meant to deal with pests as passion is to deal with unnecessary loss of interest! Passion kills the ghosts of "I can't".

108. Your self-image tells about what you think about yourself and how you appear to yourself in your own consciousness. Self-image is the picture of yourself

The great Hand Book of Quotes!

carried in your own mind. That picture can scare you or inspire you!

109.   There are some people who through hurts do not feel they are good enough and this is a destroyer of their self-images. As a true believer of your dream, you need to see yourself as God sees you. God sees you as his own handiwork and that is pretty great to carry you through!

110.   No matter how bad you feel, God never sees you as a reckless person. He may see you as a sinner who needs to be re-washed to get back to his old vision for His purpose, but He will never see you as a hopeless being who was created for nothing. Now if God will not see you as hopeless, why then should you see yourself that way? Be bold to say am qualified to dominate the world!

111.   God calls big trees out of small seeds, so He prepares great monuments out of small minds. He will definitely call those wonderful things he put in you out of you. When He begins, do not resist!

112.   I believe that we are just carriers of God's wisdom that he uses to refurnish the earth He created. You are carrying part of that wisdom in you. When it's time to offload it, do so with all passion!

113.   It's easier to maintain a good character than to recover it when it's gone bad!

The great Hand Book of Quotes!

114. Better spend time working hard to maintain your good habits because you may look for time to recover it but to no avail!

115. Good character going bad is like a beast escaping it's cage; it will be hard to capture it again!

116. Thoughts are roots; Words are leaves; Actions are fruits! Every success tree has all working normally!

117. Work and happiness are like mother and daughter; work brings forth happiness, but hard work brings forth great happiness!

118. "Pleasure" is different from "happiness". It has its own definition. Pleasure may or may not come from hard work; Pleasure may or may not come from sin; However, happiness is always divine and comes from fulfillment!

119. If hard work is the source of happiness, then we can conclude that the main job of procrastination is to delay that happiness for excuses to kill.

120. Before you point fingers at someone, clean them well. You better remove that log on your lens before you can see the speck on someone's own afar!

121. It's great to feel happy. Go, do what makes you feel happy. Do it shabbily and get shallow happiness; Do it hard and feel the hardest happiness!

www.amazon.com/author/israelmore

The great Hand Book of Quotes!

122. Sometimes you'll remove the log from your own eyes and to your amazement; you will see that your friend has no speck there after all the suspicions. You got to see before you judge!

123. One of the greatest ever statement that can keep you at peace with others is that "I am right, but I may be wrong"! Yes, we know you are right but you may be wrong!

124. I decree and I declare that I am not a raw material but rather a finished product. God knows me and knows the reason for which he created me. I am not here on earth to merely live and depart.

125. Remember, your wishes are on the ways God created. If you miss the way, you are automatically missing that great treasure! Be on the way of the Lord and your wishes will meet you at a chosen junction!

126. Pure gold does not rust. Only gold alloys do so. You may have golden dreams. But if you go in the company of toxic people, your become "a gold alloy" and what that means is that you can rust at any time!

127. For the sake of your dreams, don't create negative brands for yourself, else you scare away opportunities that are meant to be your turning point!

128. When you are happy for other people's dreams, your dreams start jumping up with joy. Elizabeth was happy

with Mary and her dream baby was jumping in her womb crazily for joy!

129. "You need to know the constituency you belong to...and that is revealed by your constituents. When your constituents are speaking in public and making of stories, your constituency can be "journalism".

130. "Attitude. That is your tendency to evaluate things based on your perception. If you think you can't, that is a negative attitude parcel and opening it will reveal what you believe"

131. "Cars are powered by either petrol or diesel or gas. That is their fuel. I don't care whether you want to pour pepper soup or orange juice into that car... It can't work! You can't live without intrinsic and extrinsic motivations and move forward"

132. "Information had become a critical tool that you can use to raise your bar across every barrier towards excellence. Deny this fact and maintain your bar wherever it was without even a lift.

133. "Information and ignorance are like light and darkness... When light comes into your room, darkness must fly away. When information rules your mind, ignorance finds its way out!

The great Hand Book of Quotes!

134. Hi ladies, Hi Girls..., If you don't add more knowledge to what you already know, you may be a virgin but may not raise your bar! Go, get extra oil!

135. The vision of life is not a "discovery"; it's a "work" and whatever position you occupy demands work. Your life may not be built on your visions if you go high and find yourself doing the vice. Going higher should be a priority; but being aware of the reason for getting there should be the focus!

136. Motivations take you there. Tell yourself you are powerful enough to make it, and it will surprise you that.. that power will start manifesting itself.

137. Never climb the tree with the reason of plucking a fruit; only to get there and pick a leaf. Let everything you get there to do be done and let it be done well!

138. I got to believe that the people who can really be trusted are those who have kept their promises, not under the influence of pleasing people, but under the influence of doing what they have devoted their lives to be doing!

139. The certificate that promotes a divine idea is humility. Period. Get yourself upgraded with the good news of humility every day! Sometimes, it's hard to prove your humility in the face of people, but never forget that it is the only option for your divine promotion!

The great Hand Book of Quotes!

140. It does not pay away a penny from you to say "am sorry", "I won't do that again"! It does not take away your integrity to appreciate the very little that you have obtained from someone, even if it's not much! True humility speaks "little is enough if God is in it.

141. God hides great things in little things. In every young girl, God hides a great woman; in every young boy, He hides a great man; in a small seed, He hides a big forest! A little is never inadequate if God's hands are its creator! Don't despise little things!

142. Never look down on someone because God himself does not do so. No matter what defines the status, nationality or gender of a person, once God's spirit is in him/her, he or she becomes a complete creature with complete potentials!

143. Sometimes, we wait on God for special things to happen extraordinarily in our lives before we understand that "God is working". Meanwhile, there are "super-special" things that fill our life barrels in minute drops, but they go unappreciated!

144. With teamwork, any little contribution you make yields greater output when it meets the contribution of others, and guess who gets the plus? Everyone in the team!

www.amazon.com/author/israelmore

The great Hand Book of Quotes!

145.   You cannot be escorted by the belief of inadequacy and get to the destination of excellence. Go along with "a can do spirit" because that is the only companion!

146.   You don't need to watch the clock once more before you refuse the company of self-disbelief! You can do it now by telling yourself "I can make it"!

147.   You are likely to vomit your dreams if you take too much at a time. Take it one after the other and don't over-eat the dreams you have! Dream big, but start small!

148.   You may work with 100% capacity every day and may not be seen by anybody for recommendation. This does not mean you should give up! The day you will decide to work at 40% may be the day you'll be seen by the person who is meant to recommend you for higher profile opportunities!

149.   It is not enough to take good decisions and make good choices. It is necessary to take heed and comply with whatever you plan and that can only happen by the influence of the Lord God, the giver of your dreams.

150.   Talkatives complain, cry, shout, brag, and are more hysterical about their lives than something else; don't be a part of that tragedy! Perhaps it's been a while now that you have been complaining, crying and shouting about your "labour pains". It's time to show us your baby!

www.amazon.com/author/israelmore

The great Hand Book of Quotes!

151. The main reason why your company can easily influence you is because "emotion and attitude are stronger than knowledge". What you see can overcome what you know. You can easily damp away what you already know when you are faced with the reality of what your senses tell you to do!

152. Change your environment and if the need be, change your company because it goes a long way to create another version for you which can easily ripe for decay!

153. The only way when your thirst for excellence is satisfied is when you take up the challenge to do a little more everyday than you have already been doing every day!

154. You are heading towards the top if you raise the bar of your standards inch by inch each hour! There is no quick way to success; it comes in installments. Every day's activity is a minor contribution to a heavy pay of success. Don't waste the day!

155. You may cry out tears for misplacing your money, but you got to cry out blood if you have misplaced your dreams. Sadly, you may not even know the great deal of influence you loss when you misplace your dreams, so how will you cry for such a loss?

156. Many losses have gone sinking daily by our inability to recognize the great deal of power reserved in

The great Hand Book of Quotes!

us. Watch out and make it real because soon, it's going to be your turn to shine!

157. When all the rays of your knowledge are brought into one channel of focus, they create a hot burning passion that won't let success escape your fences into a wrong abode!

158. Not every movement is progress; Some movements are just a way of burning fats!

159. I put complains aside and replaced each of them with trials and to my surprise, some things I see as difficult were not so before! I conclude that "Success resides behind the curtains of complains; tear those pieces of complains away and you will see the stage of your dreams clearly"!

160. Just watching the drama stage does not define your successful performance; success lies in the display you do on that drama platform and how excellent you do it when it's your turn to act!

161. Leave complains behind; Stop worrying and murmuring about the difficulty of something that you have not even attempted doing! How do you know that it's difficult if you have not even attempted doing it? Go, give a try!

The great Hand Book of Quotes!

162. Never be rigid on an action plan that always fails, freezes and frustrates. Perhaps what you need is a change of your methods you run with the peak velocity!

163. It's is not a surprising news that manna should fall from heaven in these days. But this manna will fall for those who cultivated manna farms on the clouds above! He who sow will reap; isn't it?

164. In most cases, verbal prayer alone does not change anything; when actions are branded with prayer, wonderful things happen. Actions alone do not make it as well; they lead to success when guided to labour by answered prayers. Pray and work!

165. Dreams in your life are like light bulbs that brighten your room. But having them on the ceiling is just not enough; you got to make an effort by pressing on the switch and there it goes taking away the darkness!

166. You control your life by the remotes of your actions. Anytime you take actions the screen of your life changes till you get tuned to the best station or destination of God's choice for you!

167. Life is a game where fair players are winners! But as for the "injury causers", "red-card" see their end!

168. Every game has rules. Obey the rules, win the game; disobey the rule, lose it! The game of life has loser and winners. Play fairly and win!

www.amazon.com/author/israelmore

The great Hand Book of Quotes!

169. The winners of life's game always set and have goals in focus that they score to fulfill their purposes of existence and making the planet earth to celebrate joy; the losers make life bitter for others by tormenting their senses of joy and peace!

170. Everyone born is on the field of life's game, but not everyone does wear the jersey of vision! Some people are fair players and others are injury causers; you joke with the later and they hit you down in pain and blood stains!

171. Watch out! Someone taught me that I should watch the people in my boat; some may be rolling the boat while others may be drilling holes under it! So, am determined to watch my circle!

172. Don't be selfish in life; pass the ball. Winners in life's game are people who demonstrate that they are not greedy when they have abundant of supply. They share freely provided they have it! That defines the true state of a purposeful person.

173. Not every environment accepts the progress you want to put across. Take a second look at what you dream about, be sure it can progress very well at where you are; Hiroshima and Nagasaki are not fertile grounds for a farmer's dream seeds. Go and relocate!

174. Let your hands be clean; God loves clean hands and no wonder cleanliness is next to Godliness.

www.amazon.com/author/israelmore

The great Hand Book of Quotes!

175. Feature in God's team of trainees and you will play for the winning team! This is your heritage that you will lay hands on the trophy!

176. In one opinion, the house in which you stay, the church you attend and the town in which you reside may not determine the size of your dreams, but they can influence the rate of maturity of what you have planted.

177. Your dreams can change the environment which was not conducive for it at first! However it is a good initiative for the dreams that would change one society to be nursed in another environment, before being transplanted to strive in its original environment for the change process to begin!

178. It is uncomfortable to keep your dreams in a house just behind a public toilet; your dreams will surely attract bad odours from the waste products of people in detracting environments. Keep it away from negative people!

179. Negative people talk and your dreams begin to wither off. But they begin to sprout in the fragrance of hope when they find a new soil! Change your environment!

180. Know who you are, then you can know where you can be! Choose your environment wisely; but be sure you know your dreams at first! When your dream seeds fall

onto the soil with the best environmental factor, you will have a bumper harvest!

181. Not every dream grows on every land, so you got to watch out! "Sugar cane" dreams should find the environment where there is flooding of great ideas from great people. It will die off if it is planted at the place where the drought of discouragement is a well cherished culture!

182. Waiters and quitters have a little difference; quitters begin well but do not finish it; waiters do not begin it at all. Don't be part of their tragedy. Go, make it happen now!

183. "Now-people" are winners; they say "now" and they do it now! That's the spirit we need, my friends. If you have the goals and the environment is clear enough, go ahead and do it now!

184. Don't stretch your neck to see who is not doing it; you can do it better! Don't turn to watch whoever is watching you; everybody is busily watching over his own actions at hand! Go, make your own real; do at the right time. The right time is now; so do it now!

185. Strike the rock and the water will flow; don't wait to brag about why you alone can hit the rock for water to flow; just go and do it because the world is thirsty! Your potentials are in put in you by God because he knows

The great Hand Book of Quotes!

there is a need to be fulfilled; awaken it and present it to us!

186. How I wish the police service is instructed to arrest people who over-complain! Just arrest them, do no harm to them, but make them do the "work" they complain about with hard labour!

187. If you are a "now-person", you reduce the time rate during which your success story is to be published; if you delay a bit, you are either prolonging the date of publishing or you are deleting it at all cost! Be a "now-person" and do it now!

188. Complaining is a vain way of explaining pain without gaining relief. Keep complains distances away from you.

189. Complains are like the clouds that give no rain no matter how thick they gather.

190. Don't accommodate complains in your chamber, else you have a sleepless and restless night. Keep them away and fall in love with actions for solution!

191. The blame game is already a lost game, so don't attempt dressing up to play it! Blames create no change; winners don't apportion blames!

www.amazon.com/author/israelmore

The great Hand Book of Quotes!

192.   Stop blaming people for not making you to achieve your dreams. The question is "are they the people having those dreams?"

193.   As far as it's ideal that you get helped by people, it doesn't mean they are compelled to make your dreams come true without your own efforts.

194.   No matter how you were taught by your teacher about how to recite a poem, it is impossible to wear your teacher's smiling face to the stage. You got to put on that smile.

195.   Avoid the penalties of the blame game. You were born to be boss player, not a blame giver. Stop the blame!

196.   Do it again and again. Consistency makes the rain drops to create holes in the rock. Whatever is difficult can be done easily with regular attendance, attention and action.

197.   You may have been too quick to admit the difficulty of a specific task. The question is "how many times have you tried dealing with it"? Don't say it's difficult if you haven't tried it!

198.   Stays focused and channel your little efforts through a common canal and you will marvel at the amount of pressure you create in that canal.

www.amazon.com/author/israelmore

The great Hand Book of Quotes!

199. One or two steps alone do not guarantee the evidence of your success unless you have your own peculiar definition for success. And I assure you; that definition is wrong! Do it again and again!

200. It's only "single steps" that make a journey of 1000 miles. It means the combined effect of many steps is the equivalence of a great journey. Go, take many little steps.

201. Have you started already? Keep it up! Are you getting tired? Don't give up! Did you quit? You can do it again! Great accomplishments do not come with big steps; they come with little steps taken in regular installments! Do it and do it again and again!

202. Say "no" to corruption; it does not fit you! Say "no" to bad leadership; you don't fit there. Say "no" to immorality; it will only fake you! Be bold to say "no" if that is what will take your breakfast away; you will get a sweeter lunch pack for compensation sooner.

203. I have noticed that sometimes, our success, promotion and accomplishments become real when we say "no" to some things and act the right way. The potential that drives you to do that is called "self-discipline".

204. No matter how sweet is smells, if you know it will give you a discomfort later, don't even attempt to taste it. Discipline yourself to stay out of sin!

www.amazon.com/author/israelmore

The great Hand Book of Quotes!

205.   Discipline yourself to be a disciple of great works and to do that excellently, you have to wave "bye-bye" to some things and then switch off your inner person not to go near them again!

206.   Being disciplined with an ego that makes you to feel like you can never be disciplined by any other person is "indiscipline".

207.   "Can-do" is the parent of "Have-done". No passion, no production!

208.   Create your own future; you are your own artisan. Promote your own brand; you are your own marketer! You've got the hands to do that. Just believe it is possible!

209.   Although the Bible is a living book, it will not jump into your palms pleading, "Read me please". You've to make a choice to do so!

210.   Maintain a belief system that admits that all things are possible for those responsible to have them done. It's nothing to deny; whenever God calls us for a responsibility, he give the ability for us to respond to that responsibility!

211.   Whatever negative things people think and say about you is enough to bring you down provided you belief that it carries a weight that can push you hard. Don't agree to accept what critics say; be prepared to silence them by doing what they think you can't do!

www.amazon.com/author/israelmore

The great Hand Book of Quotes!

212. The gangs of arrogant thieves that can rob you of your success are your own doubts, fears and low self-image. Get them arrested and kept distances apart and you and your accomplishments are secured.

213. "Forgiveness is a clean lotion that heals the wounds of misunderstandings! To iron out the differences; get the painful sores dressed up; Forgive and Forget!"

214. Talk to strangers politely... Every friend you have now was once a stranger, although not every stranger becomes a friend.

215. It is unpredictable for you to know which of the strangers you are about to meet that becomes your friend. Be polite to every stranger!

216. Avoid the use of abusive words when communication is in session; you might scare away someone who is meant to become your mentor or your customer.

217. Never forget that when connections get destroyed by means of bad communication, it's good communication that resolves them. Don't be shy to say "I am sorry" and "please forgive me". That's a good communication!

218. Don't be shy to say "I am sorry"; Never feel too big to say "Please forgive me"; Don't think it's unnecessary to

The great Hand Book of Quotes!

say "thank you"; Never feel bad to admit "I am wrong"! That's a good tactics is communication!

219. Avoid hating people because you might have destroyed the bridge you have just used to cross the river; you'll need that bridge to cross again when returning!

220. Be quick to resolve conflicts before they mature to become wars. The energetic crocodile was once a delicate egg!

221. You have two options to choose from as an aspiring achiever; either you become excellent or you become excellent! Mediocrity is never an option!

222. Excellence is making a rubber shoe initially; later making a leather shoe; then later making a leather shoe with gold medal on top and then making a golden shoe with diamond medal on top; going to make a real diamond shoe!

223. Excellence is a habit acquired by continuous improvement on the little things you do with a firm belief that it's going to be better than before!

224. Start lifting your brand off the ground with an excelling mentality becoming best at what you do. You can't afford to be an average person although you may have begun from a level below average.

www.amazon.com/author/israelmore

The great Hand Book of Quotes!

225. Don't sit on the fence; break it and move out! Don't be confined to the little things you do; the sky should be below your limit!

226. Refuse to become a victim of your circumstances and give a lift to your potentials each and every day against the wish of any obstacle you encounter!

227. Most people who are global achievers were once victims of greater circumstances than yours, but they had one word to sum it up; "They never give up!

228. Maintain your integrity! Live life in such a way that when another person tells his or her truth, you'll not be committed for blame.

229. Integrity involves the ability to stand straight when you tell your truth, and still stand straight when the other person comes to talk!

230. The truth may roar, but it's roaring does not terrify the blameless. Guilty conscience needs neither a critic nor an accuser. Remember, the truth has no aiding crutches; once it is limping, its name is "a lie'.

231. Work hard in the day; as hard as you can even if no one is watching you! Work harder in the night; as harder as if everyone's eyes are on you.

232. To maintain your integrity, be a person who does not violate the principles of the truth. Vote for truth even

The great Hand Book of Quotes!

if you have to vote alone; believe it "your vote will not be lost"!

233. Whatever you do well in the darkness tells more about who you are than what you do best in light. Watch out!

234. Someone may have all the technical knowledge, scientific intellect and business know-how but when he/she decides to choose laziness, excuses, procrastination, complaining and other bad attitudes, his/her relevance is meaningless.

235. Live your life in such a way that when a video coverage is taken of you either in light or in the darkness, it can receive an applause when it is shown in your chapel for everyone to view!

236. Do good even if no one is watching you and do it as if everyone is watching you.

237. "Change comes with sacrifice... When you want to make a change you must be prepared to make a sacrifice of escaping the comfort zone!"

238. Change is an institution that we all have to get enrolled into if we are really willing to make a difference! Those who are illiterates to change agree that whatever will be will be! That does not sound well!

The great Hand Book of Quotes!

239.   If you are not angry with your average performance, you can't effect a change! You must get upset to grab the energy to break the fence confining you!

240.   You have to direct change; if you don't do so, change will direct you. Guess... the direction change will offer you is not a comfortable one. But the direction you can offer change will be the most comfortable. Go, make a change now!

241.   Change comes with pain... But this pain later becomes a gain. To explain it well, "no pain, no gain"! Endure the pain and make a difference!

242.   Be an initiator of change. Keep improving... To change is to improve; to become excellent is to keep improving often! Don't give up; people who make it in life are people who keep improving often and often!

243.   Make a change! It's all about you! You may not be able to prevent the bird from flying over your head; but you can prevent it from making a nest on your head!

244.   Young man, the fact that she did not accept your proposal for a relationship does not define why you should hate her. She may not become your BRIDE, but she can be the BRIDGE you have to cross to the other side with your dreams!

The great Hand Book of Quotes!

245. Hi Lady, Hi Woman.., all that Naomi had, all that Mary had, all that Esther had, all that Elizabeth had, YOU ALSO HAVE... Go, make your dreams come true!

246. Decision is the wing that makes dreams to go and grow and flow and fly. No decision, no fulfilled destiny!

247. The deeper your thoughts, the clearer your dreams. The clearer your dreams, the higher you fly. Decide to fly!

248. I agree and admit that thinking and planning are free. Nobody charges you for thinking and you pay no one to make plans. It's your decision!

249. If you can't manage yourself, you can't manage your time. Discipline and self-control are what get you on track to execute your plans by managing your time effectively!

250. Thinking is free, planning is also free, but action taking is not free; you have a price to pay. Success is not luck; it demands work... hard work of course!

251. When you meet failure, do you decide on backing up or backing out?. If you decide to fly, you have to back up. You have to rise up when you fall down!

252. You may explore, you may evaluate but you can't execute if you are not willing to take action. Decide to take off now!

www.amazon.com/author/israelmore

The great Hand Book of Quotes!

253.   You may have access to the best information; you may build up the most positive attitude but, to get the wisest experience, your hands and legs must work!

254.   It's not bad to cough. But cover your mouth when coughing. It's not bad to complain. But cover your mouth when complaining, else you'll spread infections of complains on us!

255.   The only species of human beings that are immune to failure are those that are dead and gone. Failure is constant; just prepare to deal with it!

256.   The hopeful lenses of our eyes are fixed on the busy hands of our dependable God... He is working hardly on our prayers... Don't be afraid!

257.   Peter denied Jesus; Judas betrayed Jesus. The bad news was that both of them fell off the track and were both filled with regrets, remorse and anguish for their mischievous behaviours. However it was only Peter who chose to rise again after falling! Judas chose to end it with suicide! If you fall, you can rise again!

258.   You don't need to sit on a throne before you have the chance to dream; you don't have to feel fat meat in-between your molars to become a strategic dreamer. You can be a dreamer once you can think; dreams are germinate from imaginations; and survive through actions! Indecision weakens dreams; inaction kills them!

The great Hand Book of Quotes!

259.   The best posture you can adopt when pursuing your goals is neither to stand nor sit. The best position is to STANDOUT! Everyone may be sitting; but don't sit! Many people may be standing; but don't just stand. When you stand, be outstanding!

260.   Success can locate and visit you even if you are static wherever you are... But you are responsible for constructing the roads... Go, make the roads!

261.   The most tragic cause of social disharmony is when the speed with which people find mistakes of others outweighs their simple belief that they too are infallible!

262.   Two main definitions of a true leader; His presence is noticed and his absence is felt...!

263.   The most ignorant and wasted youthful generation is the very one that the older generation uses to create social conflicts to their own youthful detriment!

264.   One major way to avoid shifting blames unto other people is to accept and agree that the efforts that turn the loads of your self- improvement have to turn on your own pivot.

265.   You are your own vehicular machinery that ought to propel yourself under guidance of the compass of the Holy Spirit of God. Don't go off the track!

www.amazon.com/author/israelmore

The great Hand Book of Quotes!

266. Many a time, we live life without having access to the thoughts of how the hours of yesterday were spent. This comes to play because of lack of self-analysis and does not help in any way to create the excellence we claim to pursue.

267. When you live today, being accountable for yesterday, today will be better because you would have taken the chance to know the activities and people who unmade and made your day and edit today's plans for the better.

268. Never wake up waiting to hear a command from someone before you make a move; be responsible! Never repeat what made you to waste an hour of yesterday; be accountable!

269. Watch your time; keep your eyes on your talents. Set your goals and move into action. You owe the world an birth of success; Go, begin to labour for it now!

270. When the positive mind takes the lead, the legs are safe to follow without any shaking!

271. If you want to strike, strike now. No matter how skillfully a footballer strikes beyond the 90 minutes' regulated time, he makes no influence. Strike now before it becomes too late!

272. No matter how many times your obstacles hit you to the ground; you can rise up again and take "a free kick".

The great Hand Book of Quotes!

Make a good use of your rising up and take strike harder than ever!

273. A little time can help you to make a great impact, therefore you should never despise few minutes. Do it till it's done and done well!

274. Life is choice. You can choose to be who you dream to be or not to be. It all lies in the choice you make every day!

275. In most cases, failure is not determined by the obstacles we face, but by how we approach them and what our perceptions whisper to when on encountering eventualities.

276. The shark had never begged Jonah in order to get him swallowed; Jonah's own actions took him into the shark's belly! Failure may not chase after you, but when you miss your way, you will rather go chasing failure!

277. The faithfulness of the Lord is so great that no mind can comprehend it, no hand can fold it, no mouth can describe it and no experience can compete with it. All that our hearts will need, His hands will provide!

278. Never joined the wrong boat. When the destination is right, and the direction is wronged, everything goes wrongly!

The great Hand Book of Quotes!

279. Today, a lot of people, businesses, countries and even churches have their dreams sleeping in the belly of the shark where they are starved because they chose the wrong path although they know the right destination! The consequence is "becoming uncomfortable" because you refuse to let your dreams go to let "Niviveh"!

280. The moment your dreams and your revelation take a special direction while your plans and actions take the opposite direction you commit yourself into a tight box for failure!

281. Your passion is measured by the difference between your willingness to take actions and your desire to quit. When your desire to quit outweighs your willingness to persist, you are ripe for failure!

282. You can change direction if you feel like you have missed your way... Decide to do that now! Go back a little more and begin from where you missed it out! If only you are ready to rise again, you can make a right decision in that tight belly of the shark. Jonah did that earlier!

283. You don't need a prophet to wake you up from your bed; you need no archbishop to describe the size of your spoon for you. Remember, you are in the centre of management of your own affairs when the time comes for you to act!

The great Hand Book of Quotes!

284. You are the steer of your God given dreams. By the authority from the Holy Spirit of God, you will able to bend a curve where the road has a bend; you will be able to reverse your movement when the need be.

285. Success will locate and visit you even if you are static wherever you are... But remember you are responsible for constructing the roads... Go, make the roads!

286. Look upward to your God for direction! Look inward into yourself and discover your talents! Look outward into your environment and get helped! Stop looking at one direction!

287. You need God's direction before you can prosper in anything you do. However, it takes your choices to begin; it takes your passion to stay on; it also takes your integrity to finish it well!

288. God did not create you to be alone. He deposited skills, knowledge, and talents in someone out there who is expected to mentor you, teach you and encourage you to go high. Go, get a mentor!

289. Inflate yourself with a genuine passion always. This makes it possible for you to bounce back when you fall. The football is loaded with air and no sooner does it hit the floor than it bounces back again!

www.amazon.com/author/israelmore

The great Hand Book of Quotes!

290. No matter how obstacles may "play" you over the bar, you will be able to assume your shape when your passion is always intact. You will not burst!

291. You may hit the bar, you may cross the forbidden line, you may cause many fowls, but when you stay on, you will definitely get your goals being the winning goals...

292. Remember, without a goal, your stamina is useless no matter how you get trained. You may defend your integrity and attack your obstacles, but when you have no target in focus, you will score many zero number of goals...

293. It's possible to walk out of your house with "local" footsteps, printing them one by one till they go on to make "global" consequences! Go, make a safe journey!

294. Going in the company of negative people is just like having thick muddy soil underfoot... They will only draw you back if you don't tear them off! Move out of your current disposal with the intention of getting to your true destination!

295. Your bread assumes the shape of the pan in which you bake your flour. Therefore stand still and know that you can't use a rounded pan and ever get squared bread. Change the pan and get your desired shape of the bread!

www.amazon.com/author/israelmore

The great Hand Book of Quotes!

296. Your flour is your dream and your bread is your fulfillment. The environment in which your flour is baked can influence the shape of your bread... Just take it as simple as that!

297. When you are fully convinced that you are getting a triangular fulfillment, it means your dreams are being baked in a triangular pan. Never be deceived... You get what you do and how you have it done determine when you get it!

298. Prior preparation is Success divided by half. Once you have fully prepared, every hand glove that obstacles wear to pull you away from reaching your destination will become slippery!

299. People who have fully prepared always save time. Albert Einstein was right to teach that if he is given six hours to chop down a tree, he would spend the first four sharpening the axes. When you are done with your action plans, work will be easier!

300. Don't rush in order to have things done early. Be prepared before you set off. That's the rule. However, this does not mean that you keep delaying the time for beginning. You must begin by all means! Go, get prepared!

301. You are either a player or a spectator! Players influence the game while spectators watch them to do it. Such is life!

www.amazon.com/author/israelmore

The great Hand Book of Quotes!

302. Be the player in your own dream life. Don't be a spectator watching your dreams every day; Let them get going!

303. The most thought to keep in mind is that "players" gain money at the end of each game while "spectators" lose it for a ticket in order to see the gainful players display their skills. Don't you want to keep watching your dreams or you want to get on the run with them?

304. Great achievers are willing to die as hatrick dream scorers rather than to live as disappointed spectators! They keep the running to make it happen!

305. One major factor that will prevent your dreams from becoming nightmares is learning to vacate your spectators' seat and then taking steps towards the players' bench! You've got to play to win!

306. Never keep staring at the dreams you have on the paper... Don't just live like a spectator. You have the power, you have the mine, you have the skills, you can dribble your obstacles to get your goals moving to the other

307. No matter how short or long your journey to your accomplishment is, if you don't begin you can't get there. Beginning is difficult, but unavoidable!

www.amazon.com/author/israelmore

The great Hand Book of Quotes!

308. "...Working for peace is never "a one man battle". It means when one person who does not want to work for it is present among others, he/she becomes "another work" for the passionate people to work on upon and this makes the entire work more difficult"!

309. Don't lose hope... If your hope gets lost, the other side called "failure" begins to win! The quickest medicine to heal a depressed soul is to command; "arise my soul and praise the Lord". Hope is the clothe piece in which wraps a healthy soul!

310. Rise up, empower yourself and take a step. The only way to know that you still have some amount of strength in you when you fall is to attempt to rise up. However if you believe you don't have any strength, you will remain where you are!

311. You will arise, so start by attempting to rise. Don't give space for failure to erect local huts in your land; agree that you are constructing a global edifice there! Think possibility and be hopeful!

312. Never be complacent about the current steps; don't agree and follow the status quo. Be determined that you are making an indelible impact with great change. Now, dress up and go to make it happen!

313. Tradition is the prison where change is detained... To make a change, you need to agree that you are not

going with the statement "this is how we do it"! Yes, that was how it was done, but what next? Agree to change!

314. No old road leads to new destinations! Change begins when one realizes that it is unwise to pour a new wine into an old wine skin. If you change your mind, you have to change your actions too!

315. It's iron that can sharpen iron; wood cannot do that.

316. Your destiny lies in your own hands. But remember it was God who deposited it there!

317. There are no such words like "over-dreaming" or dreaming without "biometric verification". You can dream over and over again! You don't need a certificate to dream big!

318. The simple rule to abide by and become excellent is that "Don't see what you have achieved yesterday with the same pleasure eyes you used to see it when it was done by you". Look forward and do better than you did earlier!

319. Excellence is to keep beating your own standards every day. If you don't have a standard for yourself, you have no records to beat; and if you don't have any record to beat, you can't excel. What is your current standard?

320. If you are courageous, people say you are boastful or "too known". You either choose to accept what they

say to you and you need to accept it with its consequences. The consequence is that you will remain where you are!

321. You become excellent when you fly at a level that creates a wide gap between where you were before and where you are now. Fly like the eagle; the eagle flies as if it never remembered it was once an egg!

322. Don't be retarded; excellence is "status quo discarded". Look ahead and don't see the little things you do now as the final products to ever stand out of your personal actions!

323. Two football teams whose names inspire me every day; "The indomitable lions" of Cameroon and the "Super Eagles" of Nigeria. Guess; "the Eagle that is super" and "the lion that is indomitable". No wonder these teams make a great name in football.

324. Let your vision be ahead of your sight! Dream beyond what you see and never let your environment determine the size of what you see in your convictions. If possible, dream about what does not exist and the good news is that "it is possible"; so go and do it now!

325. Don't fight with narrow minded people; be determined to compel them to change their mindsets about who you stand to be, not by arguments, but by focusing on what you do every day. If they change it,

The great Hand Book of Quotes!

fine; if they don't, fine. The good news is that you are pursuing excellent!

326. Retaliation retards your excellence. Nelson Mandela would not have been named as a great man if not for his courage to forgive those who schemed and plotted it for him to spend those 10000 bitter days in prison.

327. If you think you can't make time to invest into your life at once now, you will be compelled to make time to count your regrets one by one later. By all means, you'll make time... So, make it now!

328. Vote of thanks! Our first and foremost thanksgiving goes to the almighty God, the creator of you and me, for what we have and what we don't have! May his name be praised above all other names! We grateful for a new day! Thank you Daddy Lord!

329. Don't tell me that I can't do it. Go and tell God that story. After all He is the one who gave me the air to breath and be able to do it well! Go! I believe, I can fly!

330. The only way to prevent your problem from jubilating over you is to confront them head to head with the singular hope that they will be defeated!

331. ...while some communities are chasing visions out, others are chasing one another away. ....some leaders are breaking existing records, others are breaking constructed homes.

The great Hand Book of Quotes!

332. It may be that you've just missed a great opportunity that should have been your turning point towards the direction of greatness. What next? Go into your closet and learn your lessons; "opportunity missed may not be regained, but new opportunity can be recreated with the will that have to work harder!

333. Millions of candles can be lighted from a single candle and the lifespan of that single candle will never be shortened! Feel free to share your success stories with every loved one out there; it will strengthen them but will never weaken you in any way.

334. Never be afraid to speak your mind on relevant issues; good leaders stand for relevance and they are never afraid to face the facts head on. Bad leaders see the problems, close their eyes and do something else!

335. You have it in your God-given power, the willingness to make the years ahead of you to become a brighter one. Avoid things that will not make you a success in the nearby future!

336. Don't deal bitterly with the enemy you see. Deal with the greater enemy that sent your enemy to you. If you focus on dealing with the "retailer", remember that the "producer" can employ more "retailers" and what that means is that your life business will redefine you as "dealer of enemies". Satan is behind the plot!

www.amazon.com/author/israelmore

The great Hand Book of Quotes!

337.   Those who flame up in anger against you; Satan gave them the fire to do so! Those who scratch your wound for it to pain you; Satan gave them the stick to do so! Don't hate the people; hate the man who sponsor's them~ satan!

338.   Those acidic insults being poured down on you are found in satan's gallons! Watch those who tackle you for you to fall down; watch them closely. They are wearing the booths Satan invented! Don't attack the people; attack the one who sponsors them!

339.   Do not rush to judge someone unless his/her fruits reveal the truth. However, don't forget; mostly, it's not the fault of the tree to produce bitter fruits. Sometimes, the soil determines that; blame the source! Deal with the soil! Don't deal with the tree! Other trees are there that the same soil can influence! Don't deal with your enemy, deal with the satan that sponsors them!

340.   Your character and attitude is what takes the lead in your leadership role and you follow them as a true leader". Poor character and attitude is eventually poor leadership.

341.   One of the most common areas where we fail is when we begin to think that genetic make-up of a person determines how far he can lead". Leadership is learnt and practiced!

The great Hand Book of Quotes!

342.   Unfortunately, most followers do not know that they can also become leaders because to them, leadership is confined to an "assumed" category of people who have authority or social prestige as their background pillows.

343.   They may call you "Stupid" because of what you've done in the past. Hey, you are going to be "Prominent" because of what the Lord has done. The stupid "S" in Saul was exchange to become the Prominent "P" in Paul... and you ask why? It's because of what the Lord has done, Give thanks!

344.   When we are faced with circumstances, He gives us the Power to endure! When we are faced with loss, He grants us the Poise to hold on. When we come across failure, He installs back in us the Potential to rise up again. When we meet death, He gave us the Pleasure to be carried up into the Lovely coasts of eternity!

345.   Think global; Think big! Think of planting a seed for unborn generations to taste; Think of making a shade that will provide comfort to others. If what you enjoy now appeals to you, thank God for the life of those who made it happen. However, the good news is that "you too can make it happen"!

346.   The most secretive news that can make you to shake hands with great people is humility. Pride on the other way is a dream killer.

www.amazon.com/author/israelmore

The great Hand Book of Quotes!

347. Humble yourself before the Lord and he will lift you high. People who are gentle, humble and able always have a great ending no matter how small and where obscured they have started!

348. Be humble and set the balls of your dreams rolling till God himself decides what next! As for "pride", allow it to go as a lone ranger!

349. Scripture said that "pride goes before fall". Just let pride go alone. Don't go in its company, else fall pursues both of you!

350. God is the message owner; prophets and pastors are messengers. It's happens on no account when the messenger becomes greater than the message owner! Let's us avoid these "human worships", confining our source of hope in prophets, kings, presidents, lawyers, etc. God deserves the greatest honour!

351. If you can't do it, don't pledge to do it. Don't be a liar; say only what you can do. It's better for you to have a "single sentence" manifesto about your life which is fulfilled than to have 25 chapters' theories about your visions that remain undone!

352. In His manifesto, Jesus promised to send the Holy Spirit of God to us when He ascended into the Kingdom above. He fulfilled this mission. Mission accomplished! Great people make plans and promises that they yearn to

The great Hand Book of Quotes!

fulfill. Keep your eyes on the goals you set to accomplish; let them be done as planned!

353.   Don't give up! It seems difficult to you, right? Why not do something little about it every? A little strike each day can chop down big trees. Give it a try!

354.   Do you feel like your action plans are stronger to than your capability? Just take a moment a draw a plan of how to deal with the difficult task with a single bite at each time. Go slow, but sure!

355.   Monkeys play by their sizes. Smaller tasks mostly come with smaller challenges. If you are willing to take step-by-step methods to solve bigger tasks, you will easily overcome challenges that attempt to stop you! Go, give a try!

356.   Everyday should be a working day on those difficult tasks. A little bit per day is the only way to make it through. Never feel it can't be done; it can be done with persistent actions, repeated input and consistent attendance!

357.   By stepping outside your comfort zone to do something peculiar, you confirm that you can do more than you've done. Move out!

358.   Life is a linear equation in which you can't cross multiply! If you think you can do it, you can do it. If you think you can't do it, you can't do it. It's a simple formula!

www.amazon.com/author/israelmore

The great Hand Book of Quotes!

359. I heard my teacher said "great people make history". I am not concern about "great" or "people" or "history". I am concerned about "make" and it keeps me asking the next question "how?"! They are Determined and Disciplined!

360. Love in your heart is good medicine for long live. Hatred in your blood is the major cause of heart failure! Love people, get transfused with a fresh blood and you'll live long!

361. If you can't set a better example for progress, don't show disapproval against the worse tradition!

362. Adversity kills fearful people just by showing them its weapons. As to whether that weapon is fatal or fake, they don't care to know before they surrender!

363. ...all "months" work together for the good of those who love the Lord! ...all the days of this month will work together for your goodness!

364. Don't tell me that I can't do it. Go and tell God that story. After all, He is the one who gave me the air to breath and be able to do it well! Go!

365. The consequences of giving up on your dreams are bitter than the causes of your intentions to give up. Don't give up!

The great Hand Book of Quotes!

366.   Complacency is a sword of two edges. One edge kills hard earned successes while the other end stops future glories. Complacency is a murderer and a barrier!

367.   If you drop your beliefs, you drop your success. God's mighty people begin to fall even as achievers when they begin to drop the beliefs they pursue at first.

368.   Gone are the days when success depends on how you use your muscle tissues. In this 21st century, your brain cells must work more than your muscle tissues!

369.   People who enroll themselves in the schools of pride, eventually graduate with and high degree of fall. Failure employs "prides" scholars. Get rusticated now!

370.   When you get a pinch and decide to give up, you will get a cut when you eventually do so. The consequences of giving up are more harmful than the causes. Just don't give up!

371.   Don't live life anyhow, else you get anywhere. Plan your life somehow and you can get somewhere. A slow plan is better than no plan.

372.   Just say "no" to bad attitudes. They may say you are "nobody". Yes! That's who you are; a "body" that says "no" to evil things!

373.   When I say "no" to some activities that I believe are ungodly, some people say I am "nobody". Yes, I agree…

www.amazon.com/author/israelmore

The great Hand Book of Quotes!

"no" body; that's who I am. I am a "body" that can say "no" to bad attitudes!

374. Your sight takes you where there is light... But your visions can take you through the dark places! Maintain your sight, but add your visions!

375. If you can't be the change, you can set an example for change. If you can't set an example for change, you can go and sleep! By all means, you can do something!

376. You have what others don't have. This is good news which means you can do what others can't do! You are unique; so are others!

377. If you don't know what you want, others will want you for what they know! You must know yourself!

378. Conquerors fight their own battles. You are more than a conqueror, that's why the battle was fought on your behalf by Christ. However, it does not mean you should stay idle... Dress up and go to work!

379. Your daily output is directly proportional to your daily thoughts while your activity or passivity remains as a constant. You get what you think to do provided you do it!

380. When I prepare, then I become pregnant... and then I produce. When I produce, then I praise the Lord... and then I become prosperous and then the cycle repeats!

The great Hand Book of Quotes!

381. People's curses will become your clue to win. The trash they think you have will become the treasure for greatness they will plead to enjoy! You will understand this better by and by!

382. The word "frustration" is defined as the unfortunate tendency of lessening one's destiny. Rise up and take all frustrations away! Stop squeezing your dreams into a small size... You were not created to settle for less!

383. ...21st century leaders use their brain cells more than their muscle tissues!

384. Good leaders always bring about transformation... Bad leaders only maintain and preserve long standing mediocrity!

385. His crucifixion is the key; His resurrection is the door... it is only by his death that we have the mandate to enter into the gates of eternal life. His doors are open always. Christ is king!

386. Christ is my model of leadership because he faced similar challenges we also face on earth today, but through it all He was victorious. To leaders are not overcome by challenges!

387. Whenever you feel a little stricken down in pain, think about this. The knife has to be sharpened by striking and rubbing it against something strong before it can

become useful! You are going to be great after the struggles.

388. The presence of pain should not be the reason for your low self-image. Boldness is the ability to stand tall even when the valley seems deep. Your pain will bring gain. Just believe and go to work!

389. Behind each and every difficult mountain is an easy valley. Keep climbing; endure a little more. Your pain will bring you gain!

390. When you complain, you explain pain for no gain. Endure and balance yourself through the pain, be hopeful and persist to the end.

391. I observed that most global achievers were first time global failures. It means, when you fail at your first attempt, perhaps that is the beginning of global influence. Don't give up. Dress up and go to work!

392. Let's stop discussing about who a wise person is and start learning to become wise persons. Begin acquiring knowledge at the very moment you discover that there is something called "knowledge"!

393. Democracy; Everyone's opinion is required! Autocracy; Someone's opinion is the best! Christocracy; What Christ said is FINAL!

The great Hand Book of Quotes!

394. My usual instruction to students when they are preparing to write their examinations is "think before you answer the questions". I am convinced that some multiple choice answers could be so close that you might not know the very one that answers the question correctly! Such is life. To choose your suitable dreams, you must think well!

395. Give thinking the opportunity to be your everyday meal; you get nourished by the best success nutrients. You will never be deficient!

396. You become a hypocrite when you can't freely be at peace with others, but you can carry green palm leaves to church to commemorate "palm Sunday"! Throw those palm leaves somewhere; and lay your life down for someone to walk on and get to the destined land!

397. Have a positive mentality; think it's possible. You can build on something little.... you can create something little from nothing.... and this means you build on nothing! Get something to do!

398. There is someone out there who needs just a line or a sentence of your life testimony to believe he or she can also make it. Keeping your testimony away from them is more of suspending their accomplishments till further notice! Come on! Let's learn from you!

www.amazon.com/author/israelmore

The great Hand Book of Quotes!

399. Drop down all those imaginations and feelings that "Success is built on Success". A HERO can be built from ZERO. Begin from where you stand with what you have!

400. Winners were not born winners; they learnt and practiced how to win and they have it! Everyone who gives a great testimony about his/her life begins with a beginning that was "inadequate" until something happened... an a breakthrough became evident!

401. You put yourself in a tight corner of failure if you think "it's only the rich that get richer while the poor get poorer". No! Something good can come out from you no matter who you are, what you have done and where you have been to!

402. I observed that when a footballer is about to make a threatening strike to score a goal, there comes a big shout from spectators at the field. He could either get detracted to miss the opportunity or motivated to make it happen. Such is life!

403. When you meet opportunity face to face, there will come all shouts; some are meant to make you miss the chance while others are encouragements from people who are ready to celebrate your winning goal! Whatever it is, you got to strike irrespective of who says what!

404. Never become proud within yourself when you are seen as the one to cause that great effect. Never become

timid if you know you can while others dare to prove otherwise! Mind your business and make the strike.

405. Don't feel pity for those who will feel disappointed because you have scored! You were trained not to entertain a pity party but to excel in a winning game!

406. Remember no matter how fast you run, you can't be the winner if you don't finish. As someone said, to be the first to finish, you must finish first! Go, take the strike!

407. When God opens a new page in your life, make photocopies of it, read it and share it with other people. Some may hear it when you read it, others may tear it when you share it.

408. Don't be discouraged or complacent; keep reading it, keep sharing it because it's God's page opened in your life!

409. True leaders do not make choices with reference to the opinion of the majority. They make choices based on the opinion of the truth and the truth can come from either the majority or the minority!

410. Don't be a pleaser of people just because of the fear of the losing your position. You cease to be a true leader when you do so!

411. Look at the truth from how it stands, not where it comes from. The truth is still the truth no matter whether

The great Hand Book of Quotes!

it is spoken by an Indian, an American, a Chinese, an European, an African or an Australian!

412. Never fear to lose your three square meal per day if that will cause you to be a fan of the truth. Never fear to have a decrease in the number of your friends if you should maintain the truth…

413. This is what you can do to be called a true leader; know the truth, love the truth, speak the truth and repeat the cycle over and over again and again! Let the truth reign!

414. Money is a necessity, but not the determinant of a successful life. It is there to secure you, but not to save you! It is there to support you, but not to sanctify you!

415. People who chase money without chasing any good reason for it are always brought down by the money they chase. Yes! If God gives you a gift, he adds it's manual that contains how to use it to it. However, if you chase something without receiving any authority from above, you will be tempted to throw it away because you can't find any good manual for it; Go, ask Judas Iscariot. He has more to say!

416. The truth does not need a number of supporters for authenticity. One person among the lot can be the only truthful out of the ten; 11 people out of 12 may be on the truthful side. However, the truth is the truth irrespective of how many people like to embrace it!

The great Hand Book of Quotes!

417.   Never let money be the reason why you betray your close companion. You may not have the joy to spend it because you are supposed to enjoy that money with that companion you betrayed! Do not love money; love the reason for which money exist.

418.   You may gain a position, but that does not mean you've gained leadership. You may lose position, but that does not mean you've lost leadership!

419.   Leadership is built on true character! You lose your leadership when you fake your character. The degree of leadership potential a person can expose will depend on how potent he can maintain his true character!

420.   Speak well to people; tell them the truth today! If you meet them another day, tell them the same truth! That shows how you can maintain the real character you poses!

421.   Be under the broad day light and act rightly; go into the dark night and do the same thing. Never let what you do in light and darkness mis-match. That's a good character of leadership!

422.   They call it "business" because it does not become successful by a person's "idleness". Go get busy if you want to do business; but be busy for the right reasons!

www.amazon.com/author/israelmore

The great Hand Book of Quotes!

423. We all have our unique careers that differ from one another, but the fact is that we must become "teachers and learners" at the end of it all! By the "learning career", we know what other people know; by the "teaching career", we make other people to know what we know!

424. I saw many people who begun their marathon races lately, but they eventually came up as top winners. I believe that your "lateness" does not account for your "lastness". It's not too late for you to make a start... Begin it now! No further delays!

425. Bolts work on nuts; pens work on paper. But you must work on yourself. Go, get working!

426. True leaders are like statues, whether it rains or it shines, they never bend their necks to look backwards! They never run away from challenges!

427. Lift up the weak; inspire the ignorant... Rescue the failures; encourage the deprived! Live to give... Don't only hustle for survival. Go, and settle for revival!

428. Faith has won it! Fear has lost it! When you get full of faith, the devil gets filled with fear! Keep your faith in light every day and you will keep the devil in fright always!

429. My dad once said... "Some friends are like "rubber wrappers"; they bind with you safely but get weaker when you stretch them too much". Treat your friends with

The great Hand Book of Quotes!

care, else the elasticity of their love for you may not go lasting!

430. Success has no other shortcuts apart from the ones that tell you; control thoughts, delete negativity, alternate actions and shift attitudes to become positive! Click on passion, it opens a new window for you to sign in on time!

431. Jesus is the perfect name!
He who put away his fame!
And persecuted in shame!
That you will not be the same!
It's because of you and I He came!
Believe him or have yourself to blame!
In the book of life, have your name!

432. You've to close down your umbrella when you are under a canopy. Drop your pride; give praise to God!

433. Your brand will be called on upon when it's needed. When it's not needed at the moment, keep it safely till it's call comes. Some brands shine occasionally!

434. Your names and your photos give you a unique identity. Make and maintain a good name in the hearts of people. Paint good photos in their minds.

435. Plant a good seed in people who have fertile hearts. When you are away, they'll miss you. When you are coming again, they can't wait!

The great Hand Book of Quotes!

436. Don't go in for the "yellowish" if what you need is "yellow". The attitude called precision is the quality that remarks the accuracy of your demand. Never settle for the less; Go for the exact thing!

437. Love is an admiration that comes with patience. Lust is an admiration that comes with impatience. In all, admiration is common but patience is not!

438. Good self-esteem comes from positive self-imaging. Positive self-image make you to resist wrong definitions others give about you, guiding you to live life with enthusiasm and will!

439. You may have something wise to say, but HOW YOU SAY IT may make it unwise! RECREATE it, else you'll REGRET it!

440. A church leadership that cannot provide members with business ideas should stop demanding tithe from them. Plant greatness in the members and they pay greatly; Plant zero in them and they pay in negatives!

441. Just preaching "you are blessed" to a congregation is like giving them a big fertile land. They need the seeds to plant on it; they need business ideas, a little of which is enough!

442. I have noticed over the past three years that most African Christians depend on their pastor or preachers for

directions in life than their lecturers, politicians and nurses. That tells why most people refuse certain medical priorities with regards to their pastor's messages. I think if every pastor should have entrepreneurial knowledge coupled with spiritual integrity, Africa will shake!

443.   Plantations of good morals are easily captivated, colonized and corrupted by the pests of a bad company. Spray away bad companies and you will experience a bumper harvest of your dream fruits!

444.   Nobodies are created by bad attitudes and sin. God had no time creating nobodies!

445.   Football teams that lost their matches can have many other chances to play in successive seasons; but a soul that is lost through death may not have the chance to justify its potential again!

446.   Take care of your soul; it will never lose its tournament if Jesus is the coach of your life. He will substitute your sins for righteousness and you will not be tempted to suffer a penalty for defeat! You are a winner, not a loser!

447.   There is time for everything; a time to MAKE the BEST and a time to TAKE a REST...

448.   Stop tagging everyone into your life's profile. For all you don't know, some will neither comment nor commend you; some may not like or hike with you! Evil

companies corrupt good morals... Watch who goes with you and why! ...live life soooo well!!

449. My prayer will shake heaven to come down and kiss the earth... and I will pose somewhere to watch it drop some goodies that I will later gather for my greatness. Sela!

450. Live your life in such a way that if God should greet you with "How are you?", your answer will be "I am how you wanted me to be"! Live life without regrets!

451. I can see only three planets in the entire universe, namely Heaven, Earth and Me! Heaven shines its glory on Earth and the rays keep falling on Me! I have a call!

452. The more you run away from the devil, the more you will realize that it is closer to you than before. Don't run away from it; RESIST the devil and it will FLEE from you!

453. I don't have what it takes to inspire someone to become a "worldly" musician or rapper! I can't use the power God gave me yesterday to work against the Kingdom God set up many years ago!

454. Don't say you won't strike now. "Not now" is what brings forth "never done". Strike it early, strike it now... But remember to strike it hard! Go and make the strike!

The great Hand Book of Quotes!

455.   My mama is my feeding bottle... She never goes empty no matter how deep I sip! Thank you mum!

456.   The iron may not be hot early if you want to wait for it to get heated; it will get hot if you strike it hardly! Strike it now!

457.   A Bible not read is like a bulb not lighted. Only insane people will love to work in the darkness with Kings' bulbs which are not switched on! ... and so goes the one who has the King James' but does not search into it!

458.   If it's about the strength, every big animal can catch any mouse... but the skillful brand of the cat makes it's catch exceptional! Go, get the skills!

459.   A good mother... when you CRY, she CARRIES you; when you are HUNGRY, she will HURRY to feed you; when you are about to SLEEP, she SINGS for you! Long live good mothers! Thank you mama!

460.   Give it a little more trial, a little more risk, a little more pushing up and a little more stretching out. Stretch it more and let all your ideal length be seen. Your maximum self can only be known if you stretch hard till you can't do it any longer!

461.   Don't be discouraged by people who tease you out of your dreams. What you have in your heart is bigger than what they have on their lips!

www.amazon.com/author/israelmore

The great Hand Book of Quotes!

462. "PULL and PUSH are basic principles of life. You must PULL to work hard and then PUSH to give hard"... The reason why we gain is to give!

463. If I am to choose between "sleeping" and "being part of a leadership that pursues irrelevant agenda", I will choose "sleeping". Chasing of irrelevant agenda by a leadership sect is what made Nelson Mandela to call it "Long Walk to Freedom!"

464. As a child, I used to wonder why markets in my locality were all situated near the main roads. I grew up a little to get the answer; " that business minded people can meet there easily!" Your dream must be situated where they can meet people!

465. I believe that if markets were hidden deep in obscured places, it would definitely be impossible for some people to get there to make transactions! If you secluded yourself out of sight, your dreams cannot go that far!

466. Your dreams are like the market grounds; their locations really matter. If you keep hiding your potentials out of sight, you may be great but unknown! Your influence can travel long distances if only you give them the chances to go where they are needed! Rebrand yourself!

www.amazon.com/author/israelmore

The great Hand Book of Quotes!

467.   You must always reserve a question for people who think you are proud when you talk about your dreams! The question is "how would they get to know that you are proud if you had not talked about your dreams?" How then should people get to know what you do if you take delight in hiding yourself?

468.   Obscurity makes success undefined because success is crowned by sharing what you have with people who need it; you can't share if you keep hiding!

469.   You can't be successful if you are good at hiding yourself! Be success minded; think about uncovering what you know, what you have, and what you have to know for the comfort, inspiration and enlightenment of others!

470.   You are like a global market. You can't hide yourself from global customers! Make a global exposure of your dreams and you will achieve global success!

471.   You are like a city on the hill; you can't be hidden out of sight in any way! Beautify your environment and your influence will be seen from afar!

472.   You are a lamp to give light to people; you must mount the lamp stand and shine bright! Don't hide your gifts; expose and share them freely!

473.   Keep away from people who always try to stop you from sharing your opinions with the entire world. Don't

The great Hand Book of Quotes!

listen to people who mock you because you talked about who you want to be! Exposed yourself!

474. Vacate the bench of rest and play the game of the bests. Keep on marching; no more benching!

475. Words can be medicines; they can also be poisons. Words can heal; they can also kill... It all depends on how, when and where they are use and against whom! Le us not abuse our words. It's a misuse of the tongue!

476. The earth is a planet that contains living things; I am a planet that contains living dreams! The earth revolves around the sun; I revolve around my passion!

477. Don't neglect the gifts in you. Power reserved is function suspended. The day you choose to switch on your passion is the day you will see your dunamis power in you. Be inspired!

478. Goals are easily scored with either a skillful strike or a strong one. If you make a strong strike, it's impossible for it to be defended by obstacles in your goal!

479. A child of God does not need to walk and talk as if he or she has no help from anywhere! You are a legitimate child of God once you have Christ in you... So don't tell me you have no helper!

The great Hand Book of Quotes!

480. Your help comes from the Lord God who made heaven, earth and you! Grab your mission; that's your father's assignment for you! No one can stop you from attaining success with the assignment your father gave you to do!

481. Walk on with the spirit of boldness; talk on with the glory of confidence. You have a mandated seal on your chest... When you go with a bold chest, the devil and his cohorts must give way!

482. You have authority in your mouth, hence don't need to be afraid; but rather positively affirm!

483. The first key to a purposeful living is to accept the responsibility of your mission. When you agree "yes" to the calling, then you ask God "why?".

484. You don't need to know why God sent you to the earth before you say "yes" to what He sent you for! He wants you to prosper and he is the only one who knows "how?"!

485. You may be tempted to regret being born when you are made to watch the videos of just what you will go through to achieve your dreams... But you are highly likely to wish you can live and live again and again if the size of your purposeful achievements is shown to you! Live on!

www.amazon.com/author/israelmore

The great Hand Book of Quotes!

486. Leave fears aside, clean tears away! Tell God "here I am, use me!" and he'll give you the assignments that will make your life a fulfilled one. Now dress up to work!

487. Disappointment and Depression are terrorists that kidnap people's original peace for no good reason. The Holy Spirit of God is a dependable army to drive them away! May you be free from being disappointed and depressed. May you have and share peace as long as you live!

488. My mother is my pastor
She teaches me the Bible
I love her as my mentor
She tells me to be humble!

489. My mother is my doctor
Caring for me when am ill
I will love her forever till
We are gone to our creator!

490. My mother is my teacher
Her words make me richer
I thank you oh my mother
May you grow and live longer!

491. My mother is my vendor
Cooking for me what's nice
Akple, Borbor and Rice
I can't forget this splendor!

www.amazon.com/author/israelmore

The great Hand Book of Quotes!

492.   My mother is my friend
Who shares with me her bread
All my hopelessness cured!
Her company makes me secured!

493.   If I would be made come to earth again, I would ask for the same mother again. If made to return 100 times to earth, I would request to be born through the same mother 100 times!

494.   "Your true love for God is demonstrated through your ability to hold onto your faithfulness in the midst of Prosperity and Poverty, Happiness and Hardships, Sickness and Success; in whatever is Appealing or Appalling!"

495.   It's normal for us to become unhappy for a while due to how circumstances in life treat us, but it is ungodly for us to be ungrateful for these circumstances that make us unhappy!

496.   Offence is like muddy soil; when trapped underfoot, it resists rapid progress. Don't trap offences under your mind, else you resist change! Jesus said "Shake the soil off your sandals"! What are you waiting for? Shake it off!

497.   Don't neglect adverse situations. Sometimes, they carry the yolk of great differences. When you break them away, you waste the yolk!

www.amazon.com/author/israelmore

The great Hand Book of Quotes!

498. If you don't see the images on a screen because people block your view, it is easier to adjust your sitting position than to call for an adjustment of the screen! You need to change yourself!

499. In every dream, there lays a cost to be paid. The potency and relevance of your ideas will determine the cost to be paid!

500. Having ideas is like getting fishing net; you must cast it. The broader you cast it, the greater your likelihood of achieving more!

501. One of the critical factors that make people's dreams become nightmares is that they don't know there is a cost to be paid!

502. Money is not the first step to becoming a great achiever. Your ideas determine the cost you will need to pay. So if you have no ideas, you can't know the amount you will need!

503. The mouse that makes jest of a cat has already seen a hole nearby... We don't fear the devil because we are leaning on the resurrection power of Christ!

504. As a child, I used to wonder why markets in my locality were all situated near the main roads. I grew up a little to get the answer; "that business minded people can meet there easily!" Your dream must be situated where they can meet people!

www.amazon.com/author/israelmore

The great Hand Book of Quotes!

505.   Words can be medicines; they can also be poisons. Words can heal; they can also kill... It all depends on how, when and where they are use and against whom! Let us not abuse our words. It's a misuse of the tongue!

506.   Goals are easily scored with either a skillful strike or a strong one. If you make a strong strike, it's impossible for it to be defended by obstacles in your goal!

507.   Be grateful for the life of those who mass up challenges on the paths to your fulfillment. At least they taught you self-defense!

508.   Your intelligence enhances your ability to think and recollect, dream and set realistic goals. Your stamina is built on your passion for progress and willingness to excel... When you have a great stamina, you can make great impact even with a low intelligent quotient!

509.   Never fear what people will say... Never think you can't do it because it was never done before! You can be the source of change that is suspending for quite a long period now! You too can fly!

510.   It's wrong to think that money is the first requirement for great accomplishments. This argument is neither here nor there. Money or no money, success begins with your ideas.

www.amazon.com/author/israelmore

The great Hand Book of Quotes!

511. To save your life from prodigal waste, you must have good ideas. God may give you an idea that he may send someone to pay for. Surely, if you hide that idea, you may not meet the person meant to finance it!

512. Work on your ideas with the little money you have. Share your ideas with positive people who will help you carry them through. Never give up on your ideas. Be positively minded and pay the cost involved in accomplishing your dreams!

513. The greatest tragedy to ever happen to a nation is not the incidences of war or terrorism. It's when more bookshops close down and more drinking bars are opened to replace them!

514. A country whose citizens do not read is already late because "reading" is just the first step to wisdom acquisition. Application of the learnt knowledge is the gateway to personal transformation. If you don't read, you have not yet begun anything!

515. Invest your money and time acquiring knowledge for yourself... and the good news is that as you do so, you keep your children and grandchildren and unborn generations enlightened by what you have already learnt!

516. A knowledgeable citizen is a powerful citizen because knowledge is power! Make your nation a powerful one... Keep reading to acquire more knowledge!

www.amazon.com/author/israelmore

The great Hand Book of Quotes!

Let books be your friends; never disappoint them by not studying them frequently!

517. Try to be the best; try never to be the worst! Live and play the role honey plays on your tongue in the lives of people; never do the job that pepper does on your eyes to others!

518. Your smile can heal thousands; but your anger can kill millions. Your "hand-shake" can encourage tens of people while your "finger-pointing" can turn ten thousands away from you!

519. Love your neighbor... and in doing so, do it as you love yourself! Take up the loads that will cause your neighbor a neck pain; don't put a heavy cross over his/her neck!

520. Your happiness is meaningless unless it is linked with the total liberation of people around you! You matter; others also matter! Live life so well!

521. Try your best... Do your best... Sow the best and reap the best! The best is right in you... Don't hide it and give out the worst. We are looking right up to you!

522. Words can express true feelings, true emotions and wisdom. It is up to you to use them wisely... Choose your words carefully and express the peacefully!

www.amazon.com/author/israelmore

The great Hand Book of Quotes!

523. If you can't PRAY for the peace your church, PROMOTE the Christian doctrines, PREPARE for every good work and PROVIDE for the expansion of the Church, you are just like the PEWS (table and chairs) in the chapel.

524. If your name is "canoe" and you can't float on water, you are useless! If they call you "cutlass" but you can't chop anything into pieces, you are a waste! You have a unique role, you are a brand! Do what you were created to do!

525. Yes! If you really love your beautiful garden of dreams, you will never allow any hungry beast to have its way in. Keep dream killers away!

526. When you are DOWN for satan, you'll be LOADED with sin... and you'll DOWNLOAD failure! You and I can't be part of that mess!

527. On a shirt, every button has its own button-hole. Fix a button elsewhere and your dressing goes crazy and nasty! On earth, everyone has his/her dreams. You have your own. Fix yourself there and your life will be fully fulfilled!

528. A compassionate government does not need to pay too much attention to those who don't have needs. True leadership is to fulfill a need of the needy. People who have needs need attention indeed! Be a true leader!

www.amazon.com/author/israelmore

The great Hand Book of Quotes!

529.   The shovel is bigger than the spoon, but it can never ever do the work the spoon does. They both look similar; they both have different sizes but one more thing not to forget is that "they are important in their own roles"! Each is unique! You are unique too. Take the lead!

530.   A cloudy morning does not signify that the entire day is gonna be rainy! What's pressing you down today has nothing to change about your great future! Let patience be your inspiration.

531.   "Your patriotism is not measured by what your country can do for you. It's all about what you can do for your country for your own benefit and for the benefit of unborn generations!"

532.   The darkest night in someone's life may be the brightest day in another person's life. Life rests on perceptions and conceptions or missed perceptions and misconceptions. You can choose to make good things out of every challenging circumstance. In contrast, you can also choose to see nothing in a creative opportunity.

533.   Naturally, everyone is expected to enter the future only once, but by the transport medium of dreams, great people enjoy the future twice! They pay a visit into the future by dreaming, and they relocate to settle in it by their purposeful actions!

www.amazon.com/author/israelmore

The great Hand Book of Quotes!

534. Your brand is your personal lawyer... It defends and speaks for you even in your absence. Keep calm and maintain a good brand!

535. "The ink in the pen that writes success stories is "FOCUS"...

536. "Only the legs that run are those that really have muscles!"

537. If you don't have any good idea, you are likely to waste money if it's given to you! If you don't have an idea, you can't even know how much money you need... This is because; it's your ideas that give you the cost to pay!

538. Words can express true feelings, true emotions and wisdom. It is up to you to use them wisely... Choose your words carefully and express the peacefully!

539. I am a M.A.G.I.C. child.. Motivated And Growing In Christ! ...I hope you too are a M.A.G.I.C. dreamer!

540. The main factor that makes leadership potentials to become abused often is ignorance. Many people can merely spell their names in alphabets, but cannot pronounce their brands!

541. When the weaver bird flies, nobody talks; when the busy bee flies, no one will make comments... But when a human being begins to fly, you begin to hear talks in the

The great Hand Book of Quotes!

town such as "abomination!... where did he get the wings from?". Never mind! Your dreams are your wings, so decide to fly!

542. Success is not reserved for a selected group of people who have silver spoons in their mouths. Those who have golden spoons in their hands can equally be satisfied by guiding their faiths to feed their dreams!

543. Never fear what people will say... Never think you can't do it because it was never done before! You can be the source change that is suspending for quite a long period now! You too can fly!

544. It's wrong to think that money is the first requirement for great accomplishments. This argument is neither here nor there. Money or no money, success begins with your ideas.

545. The greatest tragedy to ever happen to a nation is not the incidences of war or terrorism. It's when more bookshops close down and more drinking bars are opened to replace them!

546. A country whose citizens do not read is already late because "reading" is just the first step to wisdom acquisition. Application of the learnt knowledge is the gateway to personal transformation. If you don't read, you have not yet begun anything!

547. A knowledgeable citizen is a powerful citizen because knowledge is power! Make your nation a powerful one... Keep reading to acquire more knowledge! Let books be your friends; never disappoint them by not studying them frequently!

548. Your smile can heal thousands; but your anger can kill millions. Your "hand-shake" can encourage tens of people while your "finger-pointing" can turn ten thousands away from you!

549. Love your neighbor... and in doing so, do it as you love yourself! Take up the loads that will cause your neighbor a neck pain; don't put a heavy cross over his/her neck!

550. Your happiness is meaningless unless it is linked with the total liberation of people around you! You matter; others also matter! Live life so well!

551. Try your best... Do your best... Sow the best and reap the best! The best is right in you... Don't hide it and give out the worst. We are looking right up to you!

552. Words can express true feelings, true emotions and wisdom. It is up to you to use them wisely... Choose your words carefully and express the peacefully!

553. If you can't PRAY for the peace your church, PROMOTE the Christian doctrines, PREPARE for every good work and PROVIDE for the expansion of the

The great Hand Book of Quotes!

Church, you are just like the PEWS (table and chairs) in the chapel.

554.   Keep your handkerchief neat, and then you can be trusted with a bigger clothe. If you can't manage few minutes, you are likely to waste 24 hours no matter how many times it's given to you!

555.   When God talks, please hear… rise up my dear… drop down the fear… your future is clear… success is near… Just go and try again! Give one more trial and you'll kiss the trophy. Greatness rises up with those who rise up after falling!

556.   Defend your leadership roles with your true character. Never attack your own aspirations with corruption and unfaithfulness! Keep calm and be honest!

557.   If you really want succeed in what you do, obey this rule;… Wake up very early, go to bed lately… Occupy your time usefully!

558.   The will to dream, the courage to act and the hope to win are the stuffs that make life meaningful! Create the life you wish to live and live it fully!

559.   Live on no complex dreams… When the meaning of what you want to do isn't clear, it means there is absolutely no meaning! Simplicity with curiosity is the lap on which success rests!

www.amazon.com/author/israelmore

The great Hand Book of Quotes!

560. You can choose when and when not to be stopped... Choose to be stopped after you die... when your work is done and done well.

561. Negative people can only infest you with discouragements when they find you around... Just get lost and get saved!

562. Create a standard for yourself and not a limit. A limit tells where you can reach in life, but standard tells about what you will love to do best at a time!

563. Yea... It's impossible to lead with true virtues if you surround yourself with praise singers... people who do not cheer you up, instead of cheering up your dreams!

564. Before you go to live the life you are being forced by others to live, remember they'll never be there to share your challenges and emotions with you!

565. Stop chasing another busy self to become. Your real self is idle waiting to be lived... Go, take up your real self!

566. Success is deliberate! Excellence is intentional! Victory comes out of struggles... Winners win because they played a role... Get busy now!

567. Among the many factors that differentiate successful people from consistent failures one is

The great Hand Book of Quotes!

paramount; when failures were sleeping, successful people where thinking!

568. Your success lies behind your choices... To get there, you must choose it and drive your dreams in that chosen direction!

569. Don't forget, when you refuse to make right choices, you have already chosen to live the wrong way! Indecision is a decision to live wrongly!

570. Inferiority intentions are sample chapters of defeated stories... Courageous beginnings are examples of true leadership values!

571. You keep your followers confused when you begin very well and give up too early... Suspense is useful in movies, but useless when writing your success stories!

572. Leave no "full stop" in between the sentences that make up your life story. If anything, let "commas" show that when you were brought down by challenges, you rose up with passion and moved on again!

573. Let go of the heavy pains of yesterday and you will feel lighter to float on top with your values. Arise and float!

574. If you don't know yourself, you may easily blow away opportunities meant for your success! Know who

The great Hand Book of Quotes!

you are made of and save your dreams from premature death!

575.   Create time for yourself... There are 24 hours in a day... Outline the number to spend on your dreams every day!

576.   Before you think of asking for support from someone for the success your dreams, ask yourself "how much of what I have can I invest?" Help yourself first!

577.   Reward yourself for being able to climb up to level one... Tell yourself that you deserve a greater reward next time... Climb to level 2 and get it... Move on and on and you'll be amazed to see yourself at the peak of greatness!

578.   Never play a blame game. Your feet are aching because you put them into a tight shoe... Nobody has it on; it's you who have it on! Your aims will help you to get out of trouble games, but not your blames!

579.   Kill the fears before they endorse your failures. When you attempt to stop the terrorist at the time he's at work, you are too late!

580.   Specialization, concentration and consistency is the key to outstanding performance... Love your zone!

581.   The main factor that makes leadership potentials to become abused often is ignorance. Many people can

The great Hand Book of Quotes!

merely spell their names in alphabets, but cannot pronounce their brands!

582.   Good communication has just a little to do with eloquence. It's character that makes it more successful. Harsh words nicely articulated are sharp enough to kill your brand!

583.   You don't need to think deeply before reaching out to the excuses to give. Just lose interest in it and you gain excuses!

584.   Drop down someone else's shoe and run to take your own quickly. Don't hire your own to anybody, else it profits them nothing! Brighten the corner where you are. Yes, you can!

585.   You may be tall; you may be short. You may be a black; you may be a white. One more thing to keep behind your mind is that you "your purpose is unique". Anyone who is thinks he is clever enough will mess up when he/she wears your shoes; it won't fit!

586.   Never wear pride as the jersey of your dreams. You will miss the goal and lose your dreams if you put on pride!

587.   There are no more ceilings over my dreams... They have no limit; they limitless! They are extra-large!

www.amazon.com/author/israelmore

The great Hand Book of Quotes!

588. To become greater in anything you can do, prepare to be a rejecter of everything that you cannot do. Neglect whatever activities that do not contribute to your success and you will never regret the path you select!

www.amazon.com/author/israelmore

The great Hand Book of Quotes!

Any Feedback or Suggestion about this book is warmly welcomed. You can forward your concerns to **(+233)0244809908** or israelive@live.com or meet Israelmore Ayivor on Facebook via www.facebook.com/israelmore Subscribe to the blog www.israelmore1000.wordpress.com or www.israelmore1000.blospot.com and receive periodic messages in your mail.
Like the author's Official Page on Facebook for Inspirational Messages for daily inspirations!
www.facebook.com/israelmoreayivor

www.amazon.com/author/israelmore

Made in the USA
San Bernardino, CA
04 November 2019

59400175R00055